DISCIPLINED But *NOT* DELIVERED

Deliverance doesn't mean you don't have a struggle..... It means you have your struggle under control!

Dr. Charles R. Walker

Edited by Dr. Susan Huckstep

Copyright © 2016 by Dr. Charles R. Walker

Disciplined But Not Delivered
Deliverance doesn't mean you don't have a struggle..... It means you have your struggle under control!
by Dr. Charles R. Walker

Printed in the United States of America.

ISBN 9781498463461

All rights reserved solely by the author. The author guarantees all contents are original and do not infringe upon the legal rights of any other person or work. No part of this book may be reproduced in any form without the permission of the author. The views expressed in this book are not necessarily those of the publisher.

Unless otherwise indicated, Scripture quotations taken fromthe King James Version (KJV) – *public domain.*

www.xulonpress.com

To Bishop James Brown

Dedication

In loving memory of the late Charlie Walker Sr. and Stella Walker.

To my wife, Mary Annette Walker, of 27 years who has supported me from the beginning of this journey. To my immediate family, and most of all my church family, True Holiness Ministries, Inc., without you this book would not have been possible.

Contents

Introduction   ix

1. Exposed or Revealed   11
2. Show and Don't Tell   21
3. The Enemy Within   31
4. The Necessary Fight   40
5. License to Kill   51
6. When I was a Child   60
7. The Process to Becoming Delivered   70
8. Favor After Failure   76
9. Identity Crisis   84
10. When the Thorn Remains   91
11. A Struggle Worth Celebrating   99
12. Finishing the Course   106

Introduction

So you thought you had it all together? It has been a long time since the last time you encountered... (think for a moment). You may be thinking to yourself, several years have passed. Now ask yourself this question, did I restrain out of fear of the consequences or out of necessity? Temptation rears its head daily. You must choose to do or not to do. Nine times out of ten you don't do what you want to do, merely because of the perception it will portray to your "fellow brothers and sisters." Behind closed doors, you struggle with your greatest adversary—the person in the mirror.

In a generation where we are over churched and under saved, the finished work of the cross is often misunderstood. People understand that Jesus died for their sins but wrestle with the continuing struggle with sin even after confessing Jesus as Lord and

Savior. Spiritual success does not come overnight. Failing to succeed sometimes stems from feelings of hopelessness once we get started. As a result, we develop behaviors that appear to reflect our true selves, when in actuality we are falling apart on the inside.

The longer we endure this life as a born again Christian, we will eventually find ourselves dealing with things of the flesh. If it were not so, the Bible wouldn't have mentioned the war between the flesh and the spirit. Everyone thinks that being saved will cure all of your problems. On the contrary, it intensifies life's struggles and obstacles. What better way to overcome than to be disciplined enough until deliverance takes place down the road? Read on to see just how much deliverance you actually have compared to the deliverance that you think you possess.

"Why is discipline important? Discipline teaches us to operate by principle rather than desire. Saying no to our impulses (even the ones that are not inherently sinful) puts us in control of our appetites rather than vice versa. It deposes our lust and permits truth, virtue, and integrity to rule our minds instead." — John F. MacArthur Jr.

Chapter One:
Exposed Or Revealed?

Think back to when you were a child. Through a process that came to be known as "tough love," you learned discipline early on in life. Although surely it was difficult to see the "love" in a belt, switch, or whatever method your parents may have used as a means of discipline when you got out of line, many of us still have the image of that object fresh in our minds. To this day, we credit that object of discipline with keeping us out of jail, prison, or to an even greater extreme, the cemetery. That discipline then, one could argue, can be attributed to an object that was used to successfully get our attention, one which should shape our minds and our behavior to the point where we became well aware of the consequences if we continued to be disobedient.

What if I proposed to you, however, that while the object itself may have served its objective in teaching you a way to behave, it was in all actuality the process that helped to define and shape who you would become as a man or woman and who you continue to evolve into to this day? How many times did you have to be told not to stick your hand into the cookie jar? How often did your parents have to give you what came to be known as "the look" that signified trouble was on the horizon if you didn't straighten up? If you are like me, I didn't get it the first, second, not even the third, fourth, or a hundredth time, resulting in perhaps more sore backsides than necessary. But throughout the course of time I realized that, while sometimes painful, the process that I had to go through was crucial in more ways than I could begin to imagine in making and molding me into the man that I am now. Looking back I realize that it wasn't the discipline that taught me how to act and how to behave as I grew from childhood into my adolescent years. It was the deliverance that came about over a period of time that helped in showing me who I was, who I am now, and who I continue to become each day.

I find it fascinating, however, that, after all of the crying, all of the pain, all the correction that we endured as children, even with the discipline we experienced that taught us how to act, that instilled in us all of these wonderful values, morals, and great character traits that we can lay claim to today, still the struggle remains. While as we progress into our 20s, 30s, 40s, and beyond we no longer have to be reminded and constantly told not to stick our hands into a literal cookie jar like we did when we were kids, that proverbial "cookie jar" still has a way of showing up in our lives. It shows up in the form of a struggle that we know all too well — the struggle of infidelity within a marriage that is falling apart while smiles in Facebook pictures present the image of a happy, well-balanced couple, the battle with drugs or alcohol addiction, the family secret that you have been forced to keep since childhood that could potentially bring about damage that could prove to be irreparable. At the very core of our being, hidden and tucked away in the recesses of our minds, hearts, and ultimately our souls, deep down inside of that "cookie jar" there lies a struggle that we all, no matter how disciplined we think ourselves to be, must confront before it is exposed to those who are oblivious to the internal battles that we face every day of our lives.

Exposure — the word itself is ugly. It denotes something that is hidden, usually by our own desire for it to be tucked away and swept under the rug, coming forth to reveal that which we would much rather have people not know about us. It brings things to the light that people go to great lengths to keep nestled away in the shadows of darkness — hush money, gag orders, threats of blackmail, erased text messages, deleted call history. Exposure has the ability to destroy homes, end careers, and, in the worst cases, bring lives to an abrupt end from death threats that far too often turn into reality. News and major media outlets flock to it as their paychecks become predicated upon their ability to dig up dirt, fish for gossip, and find stories that expose celebrities and those in the public eye as being not only flawed, but living lives that are filled with scandal. In fact, one of the most highly successful and widely popular television shows of today is a political thriller series called *Scandal*. *Scandal* is based on the life of the character Olivia Pope, who is a former White House Communications

Director for The President of the United States. Pope has gone on to start her own firm which helps high profile people escape their personal scandals, all while she still deals with issues from her own past, including having an affair with The President himself!

While *Scandal* is a fictional show, many of us can also relate as we too deal with struggles from our past and our present that, if exposed, could create our own "scandal" and haunt us for the rest of our lives. The glaring difference, however, is that with us there is no script to follow, no director on set to yell "Cut!" And there are seemingly no "do-overs" when we mess up. Instead, more often than not when exposure comes into our lives, whether self-exposure or that brought about by the "scuba divers" who go deep sea diving into our past to attempt to uncover and bring to the surface things that we thought were long buried, we are usually left with feelings of personal guilt and shame as the result of our struggles being on full display, often crippling our image and causing us to retreat to a place of solitude that makes us want to throw up our hands and give up.

"*Where art thou?*" This wasn't the voice of an impatient wife who had sent her husband to the store for a carton of eggs so that she could finish preparing dinner. It wasn't a boss who had called their employee to try and figure out why he or she was running an hour late for their shift on a Monday morning. No, this was someone who was left to deal with a much greater issue at hand — The King of Kings the Lord of Lords, The Great I Am. God himself was speaking to The First Family, Adam and Eve, as the ultimate authoritative figure "walking in the garden in the cool of the day" (Genesis 3:8, KJV).

It is a story which we all know quite well. It has been taught to us in countless Sunday school lessons and preached to us in many a church service until it has become embedded in our memories and hidden in our hearts to the point where we can narrate the events with little to no hesitation. It was The Great Fall, the ultimate act of disobedience which altered the entire course of human history in ways that we still feel the effects from even today. Adam has been given responsibility by God over The Garden of Eden to take care of and "to dress and to keep it," (Genesis 2:15, KJV) only being given specific commandments: "Of every tree of the garden thou mayest freely eat, but the tree of the knowledge of good and evil, thou shalt not eat of it, for the day that thou eatest thereof, thou shalt surely die" (Genesis 2: 16-17, KJV). After receiving these clear instructions from God, The Bible says in Genesis 3 that "the serpent which was more subtle than any beast of the field which The Lord God had made" shows up and begins speaking to Adam's wife, Eve, contradicting everything that The Lord has said by telling her: "Ye shall not surely die if you eat of the fruit of the tree in the midst of the garden" (Genesis 3:4, KJV). In fact, the serpent, who we know is Satan in disguise, puts his own twist on it and says: "For God doth know in the day ye eat thereof, that your eyes shall be opened and ye shall be as gods, knowing good and evil" (Genesis 3: 4-5, KJV)!

So Eve gives the fruit from the forbidden tree to Adam and they both eat of it as Genesis 3:7 (KJV) says: "And the eyes of them both were opened, and they knew that they were naked; and they sowed fig leaves together, and made themselves aprons." Sin was introduced to a people who previously had known nothing except perfect harmony with God as they communed with him daily in The Garden of Eden, and along with that sin came exposure. Adam and Eve had been naked all along, but the awareness of their nakedness did not come until they stepped outside of the realm of discipline that God had established by telling them not to touch the fruit of this one particular tree. Every other tree that brought forth fruit was at their disposal to eat of and to enjoy. But their disobedience, that came from listening to a snake instead of the voice of The Lord, led to a fear that caused them to try to scramble together fig leaves to cover themselves in a feeble attempt to hide from the presence of God.

Does this sound familiar to anyone? We mess up. We make mistakes. We fall. Yet, instead of coming to a place of repentance and surrendering ourselves unto The Lord, we fear exposure. We hide behind the vices that we create for ourselves with a desperate hope that certain people will not find us, let alone God! What about our position in the church? What about our title? What will become of our career at the job that we worked so hard to get? Our 25 years of marriage? Who will be granted custody of the kids? So we hide. The "fig leaves" of today that we make for ourselves are the bottles of Jack Daniels; they are the secret late night rendezvous with someone who is not our spouse, the pornography and gambling addictions. *"Where art thou?"* God was not asking Adam this question because he did not know where he was physically. He is omnipresent, an all-seeing, all-knowing God! Instead, this was a spiritual question. This was not a question necessarily to EXPOSE Adam and Eve for their wrongdoing, but to simply REVEAL to them as well as us, more than 2,000 years later, that we all stand in need of a Savior, and we cannot make it on our own.

Discipline is taught, but deliverance is learned through a series of failures and shortcomings, through sin. We learn that we cannot hide from God, but most importantly, we learn that he does not want us to. He wants to strip us down from the "fig leaves" that we have made for ourselves in shame, and he wants to find us in a place where we come to complete and total surrender to him. We are his creation. Man remains his greatest masterpiece to date; you are "fearfully and wonderfully made" (Psalms 139:14, KJV) to fit the very image of God. He is not ashamed of you, no matter what you have done, no matter how far you may have fallen. Adam and Eve were indeed expelled from The Garden of Eden for their lack of discipline in succumbing to the serpent, and death was brought into the world. But from their disobedience came our "Deliverer," in the form of the second man Adam, by the name of Jesus. God chastised them just as he does to us today when we step outside of his will, but any real Father will always chasten those he loves. Let the Father love you today. Do not run from his discipline when it comes, but allow him to deliver you. What you are going through is not to expose you, but it is to reveal unto you that you need a Savior — more than you will ever know!

"True freedom is impossible without a mind made free by discipline." — Mortimer J. Adler

"People respect those who know how to admit their own mistakes and see their own weaknesses. If your heart is as transparent as crystal, people will respect you." – Sunday Adelaja

Chapter Two:
Show and "Don't" Tell

One of my fondest memories of childhood is from elementary school. All of the kids would anxiously gather together in the classroom with their full attention fixed to the center of the floor for a day that was known as "Show and Tell." This was an activity used to teach children the skill of public speaking. An object, usually something from home, would be brought to school and kids would take turns showing it to the audience of their peers and telling them something about it. Typically, it would be something that each child could stand in front of the class and brag about, something which they took great pride in showing off to everyone in attendance.

The reality of life is that now, times have changed. We are confronted and faced with things that we are not the least bit proud of. We go through trials and we sometimes come out of them with scars that we do not want to "show" or "tell" anyone. We find ourselves in places of weakness where we become vulnerable and feel open to attacks, both internally and from the outside as well. Oftentimes, we feel isolated and alone. We wonder if there is anyone that we can trust enough to be comfortable taking our mask off when they are around — to stop trying to maintain a certain image and just be ourselves. Is there someone with whom we can be open and honest with about our struggles and the fact that, while we practice a certain level of discipline daily, we remain far from being totally delivered?

Isolation has its place. More times than not, separation plays a vital part in preparing us for the destiny and purpose to which God is calling us. But I have found, even in my 18+ years of pastoring, that you cannot face certain things alone. You need at least one covenant person in whom you can confide, who will be a covering to you, who sees you even in your vulnerability. They have made up in their mind that no matter how hot the fire may get, no matter what opposition you may face, they are staying; even if it means that they run the risk of facing ridicule and intense scrutiny for sticking with you when everyone else has walked away. These are the kind of people who value your friendship over your reputation, who are more concerned about partnership than position — whether yours or theirs — and with whom you can equally share your innermost secrets. These are the kind of people with whom you can both show and tell your struggles, your fears, and even your failures, knowing that they will not expose you, no matter the cost to protect you.

It is also imperative, however, that you remain careful about who you allow to see the real you. I have learned all too well that everyone who breaks bread with you does not mean you good. There are always going to be some "Judases" at the table who laugh with you, and who listen attentively as you talk about your next move, not so that they can celebrate your success but so that they can attempt to orchestrate your demise. Be careful who you reveal too much to because information in the hands of a friend-turned-enemy becomes ammunition. Find someone you can trust, not with WHAT you have, but with WHO you are. Find someone who is so connected to you that, even if you lost it all today, they would show up tomorrow ready to remind you that you are still valuable in the sight of God, and to them as well.

The perfect example of this type of covenant relationship is found in the book of 1 Samuel Chapter 18 in the lives of David and Jonathan. The Bible says in 1 Samuel 18:1 (KJV) that: "the soul of Jonathan was knit with the soul of David, and Jonathan loved him as his own soul." These two men formed a friendship with one another that immediately became unbreakable, inasmuch so that 1 Samuel 18:4 (KJV) says: "And Jonathan stripped himself of the robe that was upon him, and gave it to David, and his garments, even to his sword, and to his bow, and to his girdle." In other words, Jonathan recognized the royalty that was on David's life as the heir to the throne of Israel. He was willing to transfer unto him his royal attire that he had grown accustomed to wearing as the son of King Saul. Do you have anyone in your life that recognizes the royalty in you? Someone who not only sees it but responds to it as well by saying: "I'm willing to give up my spot for you!" By all accounts,

Show and "Don't" Tell

Jonathan could have made the decision to be envious that this young boy, fresh from tending to the sheep, had come into the palace and immediately gained the favor of his father. But instead, because of the God ordained relationship established between the two of them, he chose to celebrate that which he saw in his friend. A true friend knows how to celebrate you, regardless of the mess that you have come out of. Before David stepped foot into the palace, he was just a shepherd boy. He was out getting dirty, running around with sheep all day. But Jonathan didn't see him as being dirty. He saw his destiny. He did not see him as who he was, but who he would be. It is a blessing to have at least one person in your life that can see the potential in you - someone who can take note of not only the "mess" that you have been, even the "mess" which you can still be at times, and, just like Jonathan did with David, still "love you as his very own soul!"

Not only is it important that you have someone who will cover you in prayer and in whom you can confide, it is equally as critical that you have someone who will be there when people try to kill you. I am not only referring to those who will attempt to end your physical life, but even more so I am speaking of those who will launch a full blown spiritual attack against you with the hope that they can assassinate your dreams, your vision, and your purpose before they can reach their full manifestation. These are the kinds of people that I commonly refer to as the "Sauls" in your life that you have to stand guard and watch out for. The "Sauls" are those people who have gotten a preview of the anointing that is on your life but, rather than celebrating what God is doing in your life, they quickly become intimidated and feel threatened by you. As a result, they begin to plot your downfall. They attempt to assassinate your character. They drag your name through the mud. Fueled by an assignment from Satan himself, the "Sauls" in your life will go to great lengths to kill what The Lord has placed inside of you before it can grow.

Allow me to give you a little history if you will. David is fresh from defeating the Philistine giant Goliath who opposed and tormented the armies of Israel with threats, leaving King Saul and all of Israel "dismayed and greatly afraid" (1 Samuel 17:11, KJV). Yet, it is David who rises to the challenge and not only kills their enemy with a stone and a slingshot, but then uses Goliath's own sword to cut off his head! It is then that, upon returning from the slaughter of the Philistine, the Bible says that a celebration ensues "and the women answered one another as they played, and said, Saul hath slain his thousands, and David his ten thousands" (1 Samuel 18:7, KJV)! It was from there that jealousy rose up in Saul as the Bible says: "And Saul eyed David from that day and forward" (1 Samuel 18:9, KVJ). Saul envied David so much — the same man he had once loved— that he began to seek his life!

In spite of Saul's envy towards David, even amidst attempted murder, 1 Samuel 19:2 (KJV) says: "But Jonathan Saul's son delighted much in David: and Jonathan told David, saying, Saul my father seeketh to kill thee: now therefore, I pray thee, take heed to thyself until the morning, and abide in a secret place and hide thyself." Jonathan, because of his unwavering loyalty and love for David, was willing to show and to tell him the plans of his enemy, Jonathan's own father, even if it cost him everything! What would become of Jonathan if Saul had found out that he was protecting David? It could very well have cost him his place in the kingdom or, far worse, his life! A true covenant person will cover you no matter the cost. If it has the potential of bringing you harm, they will tell you secrets that may even put themselves at risk but Proverbs 17:7 (KJV) says: "a friend loveth at all times, and a brother is born for adversity." Some friendships become stronger when the fire gets the hottest. It is in these moments where you find out if you can really trust a person to stay with you, even if costs them their place in the palace. When Saul sought after David every day and had him on the run in the wilderness, it was Jonathan who went to David into the woods, and strengthened his hand in God (1 Samuel 23:16, KJV).

At times, we all need someone who can strengthen us. That person who, even when the snakes are out to kill off our destiny, will encourage us and tell us that it is not over until God says it is over. Find someone with whom you can be transparent. Find someone who, when you feel like giving up, will remind you of how far you have already come and how close you are to your purpose. David had already been anointed by God as the future king over Israel. He was to take Saul's place after Saul's disobedience unto The Lord. But I am sure there were many times when he was running and afraid for his life where he felt like anything *but* a king-in-waiting. Yet it was his friend Jonathan who found him as often as he could, and kept him aware of Saul's plans to end his life and prevent him from ever coming into his kingdom.

Show and "Don't" Tell

You too have an enemy who does not want to see you reach your place in the kingdom, a devil who will seek after your life every day because he has already gotten a glimpse into your future, and he is intimidated by who you shall become. Satan does not want to see you delivered because he knows the threat that you will be to all of Hell if you find deliverance to go along with the level of discipline that you have already mastered. Together, with your God sent covenant relationship with that person who will never stop pushing you, believing in you, praying for, and strengthening you, even until death, you can get there! Jonathan's loyalty to David was remembered even after Saul and all of his sons, including Jonathan, were killed by the Philistines in battle (1 Samuel 31). After he became king, David asked: "Is there yet any that is left of the house of Saul, that I may shew him kindness for Jonathan's sake" (2 Samuel 9:1, KJV)? This ultimately paved the way for Mephibosheth the son of Jonathan, who was lame on his feet, to dwell in Jerusalem and eat continually at the king's table (1 Samuel 9:13, KJV) all because King David never forgot Jonathan's friendship towards him when he was in his wilderness experience and far removed from the royalty that he now walked in every day of his life.

On this path towards true deliverance, you must have at least one person who you can show and tell who you are beneath what everyone else can see. You must have someone you can trust that when you do show them, they will not tell anyone else what you have confided in only them. You may not be proud of it, but at least you will know that your struggles, your innermost secrets, are safe. You know that even in disagreements or times of great conflict, they will not use what you have shared with them as ammunition to expose you, but they will protect you. Most importantly, they will love you, at all times. The English poet John Donne once said: "No man is an island unto himself." When you find yourself feeling alone and like you are sinking, sure enough you need God to rescue you, but you also need someone to throw you a lifeline who you can have physical contact with here on earth. You need someone who can show you where you have lost your way and who will not tell anyone else where you may have fallen short, but who will do whatever it may take to help steer you back to the path of your complete healing and deliverance!

"Let's take off the masks and get real so we can get it right with God." — *Undena Y. Leake Jackson*

"In all of us, even in good men, there is a lawless wild-beast nature, which peers out in sleep." —Socrates

Chapter Three:

The Enemy Within

Do me a favor if you will. Find the closest mirror to you, and stand in front of it for about eight seconds so that you can clearly see your reflection. Now, strike the mirror with your hand. Do it again, one more time. Did anything happen? Depending on how hard you hit the mirror, likely all that came about from it was a moment of pain from the impact. This was simply a natural demonstration, but in the spiritual realm, this is what we do every day. We try to fight the person that we see staring back at us because often, our greatest enemy is not someone else, but it is ourselves. We face internal struggles that cripple our confidence and sabotage our self-esteem, and we often begin to wage a war against who we are until ultimately, we beat ourselves up to the point where we are left with a greater sense of agony and pain than we could ever encounter from any outside force. This, in turn, becomes yet another hindrance in our quest for deliverance.

There are things that we all go through which can make us question our worth and wonder if we are good enough to be used for the glory of God — the sting that still lingers from divorce papers where the ink is just freshly dried, the haunting memories of molestation that still follow us to this day, and even our secret sins that we have yet to find total deliverance from. Many times, it is these scars we carry with us that we find ourselves staring at, often crying over, as we wonder how a perfect God could ever find beauty in what we perceive to be our ugly imperfections. It becomes even worse when the scars are self-inflicted. When we look in the mirror and we feel as if the bruises that we have suffered in the midst of our battles have come about because of our own wrongdoing, or as a result of us failing God. "I should be further along in life than where I am right now." "If only I had gone back to school sooner things would be better." "I thought by now I would be married and have a family of my own." "I figured

I would be financially stable at this point of my life, but I'm still living paycheck to paycheck." These are some of the battles that we constantly face, not with our neighbors, the people on the job, or with our church members, but with the man (or woman) in the mirror!

It is no wonder then that deliverance seems to evade us. Right when it seems we are about to break free, something grabs tightly to our minds and threatens to keep us enslaved to the chains from our past. Because, after all of the dancing and shouting that we do in church, the running up and down the aisles, the tears that we leave on the altar, we go home and we find that we are "sleeping with the enemy" in the form of the *"inner me"* that we are left to deal with when we get all alone to ourselves. It is this *"inner me,"* who we wrestle endlessly with, that leads us into spiritual fights which in turn lead to "natural disasters." It leads us to the storms of life that, if we are not careful, we can easily find ourselves lost with seemingly no path to deliverance.

What if I told you, however, that "losing yourself" may not necessarily be a bad thing? Allow me a moment of transparency. Not too long ago, my health became a real issue. After many years of ministry, preaching to, praying for, and leading the people of God, I reached a breaking point. I found myself being exposed to things that I had not previously encountered, and I can remember just sitting in my office, hearing the praise unto God breaking forth in the midst of the sanctuary, while crying out to The Lord as I was seemingly breaking down on the inside. I knew that I was in the right place spiritually, but on top of other issues that had presented themselves, I was ashamed of who I had become physically. I remember the struggle of attempting to find a scale that I could afford that would be able to weigh me and once I finally did, looking at it with sheer disgust in myself as it showed that I weighed over 420 pounds! Stress, depression, and anxiety had created for me a reflection of a man who I had not previously viewed myself as. The morbidly obese man who was clearly visible to everyone else had been created by the enemy within where the pain was birthed, and I knew that it was time for a change. I knew then that it was time for me to face the enemy inside of me head on and to reclaim my identity!

With the help of The Lord, and with a strict diet and exercise, walking an average of 15 miles weekly and drinking 8 bottles of water a day, I can proudly share with you that at the time of writing this chapter, I am now 275 pounds, with a commitment to maintaining a healthy lifestyle! (To God belongs the glory!) In many ways, this was the man that I found through the man that I lost so in essence, "losing myself" was not a bad thing. Although little did I know that the celebration for my lifestyle change would soon be interrupted by a reality that would threaten my life in ways that I could not have imagined. Right when I was beginning to feel good about myself, just as I was starting to rejoice in the victory from the pounds that I had shed, another enemy had begun to grow inside of me. In 2012, I went to the doctor for a routine physical where I was informed that my PSA blood count was elevated. A biopsy revealed that I had prostate cancer. Imagine my initial reaction! I was well on my way to being delivered from the insecurities that had followed me — even from when I was a child and was always called "fat boy," up until an adult, feeling out of place, even in the pulpit with my peers, because of my weight — only to now discover that a new enemy had reared its ugly head in the form of cancer. Have you ever felt like you have conquered one thing and won a major battle only to have something else show up that you don't know where you will find the strength to fight, especially after you have already expended so much energy fighting the previous enemy? Have you ever had brand new, fresh wounds opened up while the others were still healing? This was where I found myself, triumphing in one major area of my life, only to be threatened to be defeated and taken out by something else.

To God be all of the glory, thankfully the cancer was detected in a timely manner and as of release of this book, after a surgery to correct the issue, I am now 100% cancer free! Let me take this time to urge every male, especially black males, to get tested. Studies show that African American men are more likely to develop prostate cancer and nearly 2.4 times as likely to die from the disease. Most are not symptomatic and will never even know that they have it without going for a checkup. Early detection can save your life. It did for me, and I am thankful to God all that remains as the evidence that I had to endure the fight with this particular enemy is a scar.

What "scars" remain in your life? What still lingers to remind you of the fight that you had to go through and may still be facing, even today? He abused you both mentally and physically and then walked out leaving you to raise the kids alone, yet you still smell the scent of his favorite cologne when you walk past the bathroom; *Scars*. You gave your all to that job and they laid you off without a moment's notice, yet you still have the paperwork on your kitchen table from the project that you were ready to passionately devote yourself to; *Scars*. I shared these few intimate details of my story with you, not to seek attention or sympathy, but to encourage you that, as crazy as it may sound, *there is beauty in your scars*. There is a certain discipline that you learn from being scarred because a real scar has a way of limiting you. It will slow you down, and it will cause you to reevaluate everything. Nothing grabs hold to your attention like a scar that you have to face and be honest with yourself every day about where it originated from.

Here I was, scarred from things associated with ministry that represented pain, scarred from the personal feelings about the weight that I had carried for so long on my body, and now scarred physically from the surgery. Only as strange as it may seem, I cherish this scar because while the other scars represented my pain, this one is symbolic of my purpose. This one serves as a reminder to me every time I look at it, that when God has a purpose for your life, the enemy cannot stop it! While it may be visible, it does not stand in the way of the victory that The Lord has given me, and I can celebrate my scars and say just like David in Psalms 119:71 (KJV): "It was good for me that I have been afflicted!"

As I mentioned earlier in this chapter, many of our scars are self-inflicted. They are brought about, many times, by things that often started out small and then, much like my weight problem, grew even larger until they became giants in our lives. In reality, most times those giants started out as mere issues that we fed, little by little, until they became bigger than us. Stop feeding the enemy that is on the inside of you with doubt, and it will soon die. More importantly, we begin to gain the victory over the enemy within us when we realize that we cannot find recovery without the scars. Scars are, in many ways, a prerequisite to attaining the deliverance that we so desperately long for. It is time for you, once and for all, to stop fighting yourself over what you refuse to allow yourself to heal from. Embrace your scars. Without them you wouldn't be who you are now and who those very same scars are helping you to become!

"It's a saying they have, that a man has a false heart in his mouth for the world to see, another in his breast to show to his special friends and his family, and the real one, the true one, the secret one, which is never known to anyone except to himself alone, hidden only God knows where." — James Clavell

"FEARLESS is getting back up and fighting for what you want over and over again....even though every time you've tried before you've lost."
— Taylor Swift

Chapter Four:
The Necessary Fight

When I was going through post-op recovery from my surgery, I was placed under strict doctor's orders not to do much of anything for 4-6 weeks. This meant that I had a lot of free time on my hands, and anyone who knows anything about the life of a full-time pastor knows that to have free time is far from a usual occurrence! To not be inundated with phone calls, board meetings and sermon preparation during that period of transition in my life created within me a bit of a "shock factor" because I was missing being able to just "be there." I have always had a passion for helping people, but with the urging of the doctor (and of course, my wife!) I had to force myself just to be still so that I could fully recover.

One of the things that this time allowed me to do, however, was to catch up on a favorite leisure activity of mine that I rarely got the opportunity to enjoy anymore — watching movies. I have always been a fan of the *Rocky* series starring Sylvester Stallone as Rocky Balboa, an undersized, underdog boxer who always faces tremendous odds, both in and outside of the ring. Through pure will and determination, with a refusal to lose, Rocky always finds a way to come out on top. I was elated then to learn that my son had the entire DVD collection and, with a little bit of persuasion, I got him to temporarily part with one of his most prized possessions (Much like his dad he is a big kid at heart!). Thanks to my son, I was able to spend some of my recovery time being nostalgic and delving into the series, while also gaining a bit of revelation from one of the movies.

In the fourth installment of the films, a highly skilled, 6'5, 261 pound Soviet boxer by the name of Ivan Drago arrives in the United States with his wife and a team of trainers from the USSR and Cuba. After being highly touted by his manager for his athleticism and superior ability, Rocky's former foe-turned-best friend, Apollo Creed, challenges Ivan Drago to an exhibition match. Reluctantly, Rocky agrees to train Apollo for the fight, sensing that Apollo is doing it just to prove to himself that he still has it. At one point Rocky even asks his friend if this is really: "you against you?" Talk about the enemy within that I referred to in the previous chapter! Sometimes the fight that we are in is a direct result of us feeling like it is necessary just to prove to ourselves, after we have gone through so many intense battles, that we still have some fight left in us and that, contrary to what many people may choose to believe, we are not finished just yet!

By the end of the first round, Apollo has already taken such a beating that Rocky and his regular trainer plead with him to throw in the towel and give up, but he insists that they not stop the fight. This ultimately leads to the fatal blow from Drago in Round 2 that ends his life right in the ring. Moments after, as doctors tend to Apollo and Rocky holds his dying friend in his arms, cameras and reporters surround the Russian fighter. Drago looks in the direction of Rocky and says with no remorse: "If he dies, he dies!" As Rocky lifts up his head and hears these words, it

The Necessary Fight

becomes apparent that watching his best friend die at the hands of a man who clearly had cruel intentions going into the match now makes a fight with Drago not only inevitable, but necessary. Have you ever had to watch something that you love, that which you held close to your heart, just die? A little boy who is reared in a broken home can relate to this all too well —cancelled father and son fishing trips, missed birthday phone calls, conversations about life lessons that never take place. Eventually many males, (particularly, young black males) grow into adults and have children of their own, vowing not to repeat the same mistakes of a relationship with their father that they were forced to watch die. To be a better man, a better example to their own son or daughter becomes a daily fight that they find to be absolutely necessary. There are many cases of past encounters that we often both witness and experience for ourselves which ignite a fire within us to make sure that we fight as hard as we can to avoid having to watch that which we view as most precious, most valuable to us, just die.

There are times, however, that even when we know we must fight, when it becomes our only viable option, that the circumstances surrounding the fight, the opposition that stands before us, still makes the fight very scary. We watch how the cancer took out those closest to us, but the reality and often, the finality of it does not hit us until the long hours of chemotherapy begins for us. We see how the divorce affected the family down the street, but the full effects of the pain do not show up until we see the tears in our own kids' eyes after the custody hearing has come to an end. It is one thing to read about someone else's fight in the morning newspaper, or to hear about another person's fight at the water cooler at work, but you do not truly know the magnitude of a fight until it comes to your front door, until it hits home in a way that lets you know that now you are left with no other choice but to respond and to fight back. It was the former World Heavyweight Boxing Champion Mike Tyson who once said: "Everybody has a game plan until they get punched in the mouth." There are some fights that you go through that will cause you to step back and reevaluate your plan of attack, forcing you to rethink your entire strategy and causing you to question whether or not you are even equipped or ready for what is now proving to be the fight of your life.

Even in the movie, after Rocky had already made the decision that it was necessary for him to avenge Apollo's death in the ring, his wife, Adrian, moved by fear, looked at her husband and said: "It's suicide; you've seen him (Drago). You know how strong he is. You can't win!" While she was simply showing genuine concern that the same fate which befell Apollo might await Rocky, there are times when you know that it is imperative for you to fight, not just for yourself, but for others who are depending on you. There are moments when, although you appreciate the concern, you know that you have to block out all of the doubters. You have to silence the noise from the critics and haters, and do what you know is necessary for you to do!

One of the greatest examples of being involved in a necessary fight can be found in the book of Job. The Bible says: "there came a day when the sons of God came to present themselves before the Lord and Satan came also among them. And the Lord said unto Satan, "Whence comest thou?" Then Satan answered the Lord, and said, "from going to and fro in the earth, and from walking up and down in it." And the Lord said unto Satan, "hast thou considered my servant Job, that there is none like him in the earth, a perfect and an upright man, one that feareth God and escheweth evil" (Job 1: 6-8, KJV)? In other words, God recommended Job as being the number one contender for the fight that Satan was looking for! Satan then asks God: "Hast thou not made a hedge around him, and about his house, and about all that he hath on every side? Thou hast blessed the work of his hands and his substance is increased in the land. But put forth thine hand now, and touch all that he hath, and he will curse thee to thy face" (Job 1: 10-11, KJV). So, God gives Satan permission to take away everything that Job has and one right after another, messengers come to tell him that his cattle were stolen away, his servants were killed, and even his own children had died. Talk about a bad day! Remarkably though, Job 1:22 (KJV) says: "In all this Job sinned not, nor charged God foolishly!" Satan then comes back a second time and receives permission from the Lord to attack Job's body, with the stipulation attached that he cannot take his life. He afflicts him with "sore boils from the top of his head to the sole of his foot" (Job 2:7, KJV). After getting so bad off, Job 2:8 (KJV) says "and he took him a potsherd to scrape himself withal; and he sat down among the ashes." Finally his wife has seen enough and urges Job to: "Curse God and die!" (Job 2:9, KJV). Sounding much like Rocky's wife, Adrian, she was essentially saying: "This is a fight that you cannot win!" It was Job's relationship with God, however, that quickly caused his response to her: "Thou speakest as one of the foolish women speaketh!" (Job 2:10, KJV). In other words, he was saying: "Woman, you are talking crazy!" The fighter in him refused to allow him to abandon his faith in God and as the latter part of Job 2:10 says: "In all this did not Job sin with his lips."

It is your relationship with God that will sustain you, even during the fight. Even when some of the people closest to you feel like it doesn't make sense for you to still be fighting, to still be holding on, it takes knowing God will bring you out, and trusting that, even if he doesn't, either way you are going to fight. With his wife and even his friends not being able to see how God could still possibly be in the midst of his situation, Job kept on fighting. With what I imagine to be tears in his eyes, fighting back the pain, he still managed to utter the words: "Though he slay me, yet will I trust him" (Job 13:15, KJV). Can you still trust God, even during the fight of your life? Will you still maintain your integrity and serve the Lord, even when it seems as though you are right on the brink of defeat? Because Job made the decision to trust God, even when the fight wasn't going in his favor, Job 42:10 (KJV) says: "And the Lord turned the captivity of Job, and gave him twice as much as he had before. For everything that he lost in the fight, after he had endured and made it through the fight, God gave him double the blessings" and "the Lord blessed the latter end of Job more than his beginning" (Job 42:12, KJV). God will turn your captivity if you just survive the fight, one more round. You can make it. The blessing that will come from holding fast to your integrity, your discipline, during the fight will show you that for as rough as it was, as hard as it got at times, the fight was indeed a necessity!

In Genesis 32, we find Jacob being left alone to wrestle all night long with an angel of God until daybreak, with the angel telling him in Genesis 32:26, (KJV) "let me go, for the day breaketh." It was the "fight" in Jacob, however, that caused him to say in that same verse of Scripture, "I will not let thee go, except thou bless me!" When you want a blessing from God badly enough, you will not easily let go! Jacob's hip was thrown out of place while wrestling with the angel, and he was left with a limp. But the limp did not matter because moments after the fight, God changed his name from Jacob, meaning "Deceiver," to Israel, meaning "Prince with God." A *real* fight will change you! It will change your name, and it will change your reputation. Whereas you may have been known to back down from a fight before, you will not easily back down from a challenge if it means getting everything that God has for you, even if it takes all night long! Jacob may have had a limp but, thanks to the fight, his *walk* with God from that day forward became greater than it had ever been before!

One other thing that I find fascinating in this story, as I conclude this chapter, is that after wrestling with the angel, in Genesis 32: 29 (KJV) Jacob asks him to reveal unto him his name, (only fair, right?) but the angel replies: "Wherefore is it that thou dost ask after my name?" In other words, he was saying unto Jacob: "Now that the fight is over, my name doesn't matter. All that is of importance is that you got your blessing!" There are times when you will find yourself in what I call "the anonymous fight." Life will hit you so hard that you don't even have a name for what you are up against; you don't even know what to call it. But when you trust in God, he will keep you, through every round of the fight. Genesis 32: 20 (KJV) says: "And Jacob called the name of the place Peniel: for I have seen God face to face, and my life is preserved." The fight that you have been in has been intense; you have had to cry many days and nights. There have been times when you undoubtedly felt like giving up, but God has, and he will continue, to preserve you. Can I give you a spoiler? The good news is that he has already "fixed" the fight. You win! Because the fight is helping you to see God in an even greater way than you ever could before, every bit of it has been necessary!

> *"You will never be entirely comfortable. This is the truth behind the champion - he is always fighting something. To do otherwise is to settle."* — Julien Smith

> "The only limits are those you impose upon yourself. You are the one who gives yourself permission to be you. Not anyone else."
> —Russell Eric Dobda

Chapter Five:
License to Kill

Up until a certain level of discipline has been reached, there are certain things a person must have special permission to do. A zealous teenager cannot go out and drive a car on the road until they have taken a test and completed the necessary requirements to get their learner's permit and ultimately their driver's license. Even then, until they get a vehicle of their own, a teenager cannot just go grab the keys to their parents' car and take it whenever they so desire. It is only after they have demonstrated the responsibility and the discipline to conduct themselves the appropriate way behind the wheel, that the keys are then delivered into their hands. This same principle applies in many other instances as well. Permission is typically not granted to someone whose behavior has proven to be detrimental, or harmful to others, as well as themselves. Most, if not all professional establishments, require the owner to have a license. It is typically posted where it is visible to all, to show that the business is not only capable, but legally certified to do that which it has been established to carry out and perform.

Even as it pertains to our walk with God, there are some things that we cannot do without being granted permission. With the Bible serving as our ultimate blueprint and guide, we are responsible for governing and controlling our spirit man by using the principles outlined within The Word of God to give ourselves the permission to do certain things that are beneficial to not only maintaining our discipline but in striving for our deliverance as well. Of the utmost importance is seeing to it that we take the initiative in giving ourselves the "license" or permission, to kill anything within us that will serve as a hindrance to getting to the destiny and purpose that God has ordained for us to reach. The Apostle Paul alluded to this necessity in 1 Corinthians 15:31

(KJV) when he wrote the words: "I die daily." This was not a physical death that he spoke of. It was a spiritual death that he knew he had to allow himself to undergo *daily*, in order to become the man who God intended for him to be. In essence, Paul was saying that every day I have to *discipline* myself to die to things in the flesh so that I can get closer to the *deliverance* that I so desperately need! It is impossible to hold fast to the discipline that is so crucial for moving into the process of being delivered, without giving ourselves permission to begin to "die daily" to things that will serve as a distraction in the form of a sin that will ultimately kill us if we do not kill it first!

Death — it is a word that conjures up negative feelings. When we hear it, we cringe. It denotes finality. Images flood our minds of long walks through hospital floors to say goodbye to those who we love, funeral arrangements, cemetery visits. No one thinks of death as being pleasant or as something that we look forward to. It is the reason why, even after the doctor has given up hope and determined that there is nothing left that they can do, we still wrestle with the decision of pulling the plug on the life support that our beloved family member cannot breathe without. We want to hold on. We remember the fun times that we had with the person that we stare at from the cracked door of the hospital room as they lie there helplessly. We look on with tears in our eyes knowing that the hurt from losing the person that we spent years loving so dearly will soon overtake us. Surely, nothing about the arrival of death, even when we know that it is expected, prepares us for the hurt that comes with the reality that it is time to let go.

Dying to our flesh is much the same way. We do not want to "let go" of certain things because of the pleasure that they bring. The reality is that sin feels good. People may drink *because* of a certain pain which leads them to feel as though a bottle of Hennessy will help temporarily medicate. Pain is the furthest thing from their mind when they become intoxicated and are out partying and, as the young folks say, "turning up!" All that matters in that moment is the hope that the feeling of euphoria and happiness is one that does not wear off anytime soon. It is usually the hangover that one is left with the next morning that leads to the regret of a wild night that seemed like such a great idea in "the moment." Sin creates a hangover, one that will leave you with a headache that no dosage of Tylenol can get rid of. The flesh will tell you, much like the old adage popularized at the historic Woodstock Music Festival, "if it feels good, do it!" The disclaimer that it does not provide, however, is one that can only be found in Romans 6:23 (KJV): "For the wages of sin is death!" Unless we bring our flesh under subjection and align it with God's Word, we face the danger of allowing things that give us temporary satisfaction to cause us permanent pain — even to the point of a slow, yet ever so tragic, spiritual death. There are some things that simply are not worth holding on to if they affect our discipline or our deliverance and, as hard as it may be, each and every day we must use the license that God has given to kill off another part of us that may indeed "feel good." Giving in to the desires of our flesh will carry with it detrimental consequences, often leading to our untimely spiritual demise.

So how do we take control of our flesh and use the license that has been given to us to kill it? We begin by realizing who it is that has given us permission to do so. The Apostle Paul also writes in Galatians 5:24 (KJV) saying: "And they that are Christ's have crucified the flesh with the affections and lusts." When you know you belong to Christ, you realize that you have been given the authority by his spirit, not just to kill the flesh, but to *crucify* it. To crucify means to put to death by nailing or binding to a cross, just as was done to our Lord and Savior Jesus Christ. There are some things, and even some people, that we have to "bind" and "leave hanging," even some of which we are affectionate with and lust after! Belonging to Jesus carries with it many benefits, one of which is knowing that we have the liberty and the license to do as Hebrews 12:1 (KJV) says and "lay aside every weight, and the sin which doth so easily beset us, and to run with patience the race that is set before us." No Olympic sprinter as he approaches the starting point of the race does so with a lot of things attached that will slow him down. In fact, you will often see him removing things that may serve as extra weight so that once he hits his stride, nothing will hinder him as he prepares to cross the finish line in victory. So too should it be with us. It is often the "weight" that we carry with us that slows us down and keeps us from making it across the finish line where our deliverance awaits — just a little "white lie," just an "innocent" text message here or there to someone we are not married to, just "occasionally" cheating on our taxes to get a little bit more money. These are the "weights" that eventually materialize into sin which we find ourselves needing the very grace of God to come and rescue us from.

While God's grace is indeed sufficient and often serves as a lifeline when we fall, it remains far from a license to sin. Instead, we should allow it to serve as the underlying power to drive us out of sin. In Romans 6:1 (KJV) Paul asks the compelling question: "Shall we continue in sin that grace may abound? Followed up with the emphatic response to his own question: "God forbid!" Grace is not a "get out of jail free card" that permits us to abandon our discipline as we so desire. Rather it is the undeserved favor of God in our lives, even if we should happen to mess up, that demonstrates his love towards us in such a way that should make us want to "walk in the spirit" so that we do not "fulfill the lust of the flesh" Galatians 5:16 (KJV). The love that God shows by bestowing his grace upon us even when we are not worthy of it is convicting enough alone that it should cause us to want to kill off anything that would prevent us from getting closer to him, even if it means that a "self-assassination" must take place in our lives. We cannot allow anything, or anyone to stand between us and our deliverance, even if it is ourselves! We must die out to our flesh daily so that we can walk in the spirit and live in the abundance that God has for us!

In Virginia, as I am sure is the case in most states, if you are pulled over by the police for even a minor traffic violation, the first thing the officer asks for when they approach your vehicle is generally your license and your registration. This signifies to them that you have the right and the authority to be on the roadway and that you are the owner of the car that you are operating. Often they will take your information and go back to run your name and your plates to check your credentials while you wait for the outcome. In your walk with Christ, can I tell you that Satan does the same thing? When you make a mistake, no matter how small it may be, he is standing there before God, ready to run your credentials. As the "accuser of the brethren," (Revelation 12:10, KJV) the devil is constantly saying that you are not fit, or qualified to be used by God, but the devil is a liar! The blood that Jesus shed for you on Calvary's cross has given you all of the credentials that you need! When you committed yourself to him, you became the owner of a new life. 2 Corinthians 5:17 (KJV) says: "Therefore, if any man be in Christ, he is a new creature: old things are passed away; behold all things are become new." Not only that, we can find comfort in knowing as Lamentations 3:23 (KJV) tells us the mercies of God "are new every morning." You may have messed up and fallen short in the past, but God's mercy and grace continues each day to give you a renewed license to kill off any part of your flesh that will hinder you from drawing closer to God. Walk in it today! Use your license to kill so that you can not only live, but live more abundantly by walking in the victory that The Lord desires to give to you by way of the deliverance that he has already granted you the permission to have!

> *"Many times we are our worst enemy. If we could learn to conquer ourselves, then we will have a much easier time overcoming the obstacles that are in front of us."*
> —Stephan Labossiere

"Most people don't grow up. Most people age. They find parking spaces, honor their credit cards, get married, have children, and call that maturity. What that is, is aging." —Maya Angelou

Chapter Six:
When I Was A Child

Recently I was cleaning out the attic when I stumbled across something that brought all kinds of memories back to my mind. Tucked away in the corner, buried beneath blankets, scrapbooks, and even a few cobwebs was a toy box that had not been opened since my son, now a grown man, was running around with snotty noses and poked out bottom lips from not getting his way at times. It was after I opened it up that a feeling of nostalgia really came over me. I may have even struggled to fight back a tear or two as I looked over the action figures, matchbox cars and toys that once entertained my now 34-year-old son who

I gladly took in at the age of three and became a father to. Things that kids of today would find to be outdated and boring in this era of Xboxes, PlayStations and iPads were once the very things that some boys got great joy out of playing with for hours on end. But, I found from my own observations that time does indeed bring about a change.

The toys that keep children occupied at the age of five fail to hold their attention span or continue to provide fun for them by the time they turn ten. Likewise, at the age of 16 the fascination goes from wanting to ride bikes to being ready to learn how to drive an actual car. It is the evolution of life, the process of maturation that takes a child into adulthood and causes them to outgrow things both physically and mentally. They are no longer satisfied because they know there is something more, something greater, to aspire to. It happens to us all, whether male or female. There are many things which we eventually find ourselves "too old" for as we reach a certain level, physically and mentally. The problem I find is that it is often a failure to reach that all important third level of maturity that continues to hold us back and stunt our growth. We fail to grow into a place spiritually where we no longer find ourselves entertained by, or entertaining certain things.

Paul says in 1 Corinthians 13:11 (KJV): "When I was a child, I spoke as a child, I understood as a child, I thought as a child: but when I became a man, I put away childish things." There are at least three interesting things to note here. He says, "I spoke as a child." Try having a conversation about the architectural design of a building with a five year old. You will quickly learn that your attempts at discussing the construction and layout of the building with a child are futile, and you will likely encounter more than a few confused looks. Talk to this same little boy about where a Lego block goes, and he will probably be able to both explain and show you where the piece belongs. That is because the toy is more suited to his level of conversation. Unlike the construction of a 50-foot high steel building, it is something he can relate to. Until a child's vocabulary increases with age and their speech becomes more enhanced, you can only expect them to speak a certain way. No matter how smart or advanced they may appear to be, giving a ten year old the task of delivering a speech on the state of foreign policies will, more than likely, lead to disaster. There are levels which one must go through to become mature and capable of speaking as an adult.

Secondly, Paul says: "I understood as a child." I don't know about you, but I used to have a hard time as a child figuring out why my momma would say things like: "Son, eat all of your vegetables and the food on your plate before you can have dessert." Naturally, as a child I wasn't thinking about the spinach in front of me. My mind was on that big piece of chocolate cake sitting off to the side that I couldn't take my eyes off of. She understood that which I was unable to as a child. If I ate the cake first then I would no longer have an appetite for the real food that was needed in order for my bones to get stronger and for me to grow. Furthermore, I could not grasp at the time that eating too much cake before eating the meat and vegetables had the potential of causing me pain in the form of a stomachache that could have been avoided altogether. My mother, in her adult mind and from experiences of her own, was able to understand these things that I could not as a child. She was protecting me from irrational decisions that I would have made as the result of my own immaturity.

Lastly, he says: "I thought as a child." It seems as if every child goes through a phase at some point or another, whether from watching too many cartoons or becoming too engrossed in the world of "make believe" in their heads, of thinking they can fly. Well, I remember my first experience of "thinking I could fly" as an eight year old. It started with the phrase: "Look, I'm Superman" as I jumped out of a tree, my leg was caught on a protruding branch exposing the pulsating white meat — realizing that I indeed, could not fly. I'm sure the looks that my mother and father gave me when they got that hospital bill made me wish that I had the ability to temporarily fly away.

Finally, Paul concludes the verse with this statement filled with such a sobering reality: "But when I became a man, I put away childish things." Basically he said, "I grew up." It happened to me too. Now, if you were to try to speak to me about Lego blocks, it is a conversation that I can no longer relate to because I have moved on to talking about a sure foundation in Jesus Christ on whom I stand. These days, I understand that even though some things may look good and may be satisfying to the flesh, I cannot eat everything that is set before me. It will be hard to digest if I do not allow the meat of the Word of God to curb my appetite for things that ultimately mean me harm both naturally and spiritually. I now realize that if I jump out of a tree, I cannot fly, but I know that in God I can ascend to heights that know no limits or boundaries. The reason why that box of toys filled with things that my son once took great pleasure in playing with was stashed away in the corner in the attic was because it had been "put away." Even right now, if I were to just pull out one of those toys and go to him and say "Son, let's play," he would in all likelihood, look at me like I had lost my mind.

How easy it is for us to find ourselves putting away things that no longer captivate our attention or satisfy our desires as we grow mentally and physically, but why is it that we sometimes see within ourselves a struggle to put away certain things so that we might grow to a place of maturity on a spiritual level? We have no problems living holy when we are around our fellow church members on Sunday or as we meet for various services throughout the week, but we often lack that same discipline when we come in contact with friends or colleagues on the job. We sing the praises of The Lord loud in the sanctuary, but no sooner than we get out of service we fly off the handle and curse that person out who cuts us off in traffic on the way home, "Childish things." Being spiritually mature means that we grow to a place where we no longer react to certain situations the same way we would have before we, as Paul says, "became a man." Particularly among leaders, one thing that I often stress is that you must learn to keep your composure, even in the midst of storms when everything around you seems to be falling apart. Children are notorious for throwing temper tantrums when things don't go how they want them to, but fully grown adults learn how to respond to chaotic moments and to just deal with it. It is hard to lead anyone else into battle when you find yourself so easily rattled by the least little thing. This does not mean that you will always make the perfect decision when encountering a conflict, nor does it imply that there will not be moments when you find yourself weak and perhaps even making a mistake and exhibiting behavior that you look back on after the fact as having been "childish." It simply speaks to the fact that you will not resort to rolling around in the floor and throwing a fit when things go wrong as a child is so quick to do, but you will ultimately revert back to the discipline that reveals that you are better than that. Thinking as, understanding as, and speaking as a child should no longer be a habit once you begin to put discipline into practice, demonstrating a desire to be delivered from that child-like mentality.

One of the particular reasons why I love the writings of the Apostle Paul as much as I do, is because through his life we see a great deal of the transparency that many of us could benefit from today. In order to gain a greater understanding of his "when I was a child..." dialogue, we need not go back any further to the telling words that he wrote in Romans 7:19 (KJV): "For the good that I would I do not: but the evil which I would not, that I do." Here, he is speaking of his struggles and letting it be known that there are times when he misses the mark. In other words he is saying, "More times than not, I don't do the things that I should, and I find myself doing a lot of the things which I know I should not be doing." It is this openness and honesty that shows us that he has not yet reached the place of maturity that he had attained when he wrote the words "but when I became a man, I put away childish things," or the ever so powerful Scripture found in Philippians 4:13 (KJV): "I can do all things through Christ who strengthens me." No one, no matter how saved they may think themselves to be, reaches this point overnight. Even Paul, who went on to write two thirds of the New Testament came to realize that it is a process, one that may sometimes be filled with failures, setbacks, tears and trials, to becoming not only disciplined, but delivered. The resulting transformation will prove to have been so worth it once that place of maturity in Christ is finally reached.

Just as my son had to transition from a child into an adult, I now experience the joys each day of watching him as he continues to evolve into a great father. I sit back and smile as I see a direct reflection of Shaunte' in the life of his son, Te'Shaun, who walks, talks, and, in many ways, acts just like him, often repeating some of the same mistakes that he made at that age. It is the evolution of life. There will be bumps and growing pains, but it is preparation for the process of growing up — going from a son, to becoming a father. I am reminded of the R&B group Boyz II Men that dominated the charts in the early to late nineties. Their name alone suggested that they knew what it was like to go from immature, to mature. They knew what it was like to struggle, to still not quite have it all together, but making the necessary changes and

When I Was A Child

prioritizing to the point where they would not allow anything to stunt their growth and prevent them from becoming successful. What is holding you back from becoming all that God has already predestined you to be? What is stunting your growth and slowing your progress to the point where you keep on repeating the same mistakes, wandering around in the wilderness and delaying the destiny that The Lord is anxiously waiting to see you get in position to reach? What is preventing you from graduating from being a "son" to becoming a "father?" You may not even have any biological children but I can assure you of this: Someone is watching you. Someone is looking to you for leadership and guidance. Lead them. Show them the way by aligning yourself and getting in position in God to where you can say that you are mature. Show them that you have become a man, and that, once and for all, you have put away childish things.

"Growing old is mandatory. Growing up is optional." —Cindy Gerard

"*Muddy water is best cleared by leaving it alone.*" — Alan W. Watts

Chapter Seven:
The Process to Becoming Delivered

Most people cringe at the thought of process. We live in a results oriented society where people want to see instant progress. The invention of self-checkout lines, having easy access to things that we need via apps on our cell phones and countless other means of technology have put everyone in a hurry to skip the process and go straight to getting things done. While a lot of these things serve as a great convenience by cutting down on the amount of time that it takes to complete certain tasks, one thing that there is no shortcut around, no easy way to take in dealing with, is deliverance. Usually when we think of a need to be delivered, it is associated with something that a person has struggled with for years. Often there are certain generational curses that have been prevalent in a family for so many years that these demonic spirits have established a territory and set up strongholds that are not easy to tear down. While some struggles prove themselves to be easy to overcome, there are things that we sometimes feel we have gotten beyond, only to realize that we just simply have not been faced with what we know to be our greatest fight. Indeed, it is quite easy to say that you have been delivered from the spirit of lust until your strength is put to the test entering a nudist camp. You can be equipped with a Bible and feel as though you have on the "full armor of God," but it is only when confronted with your weakness that you learn whether you have truly made progress or if you are still undergoing the process of attaining your deliverance in a particular area. This is why until we are sure that we have reached a place where we can look our biggest enemy square in the eye and not flinch or back down, we must know our limitations and respond to them accordingly.

You will only know true deliverance when you stand face to face and come head on with your greatest test. There are times in life when, because of an uninterrupted span of normalcy, we celebrate what we cannot perceive to be at the time, a false sense of deliverance. A person can go on and on boasting and bragging about how they can swim on a level comparable to that of Olympic gold medalist Michael Phelps. However, throw them in the water and you will see differently when they struggle to barely even stay afloat. Again, you only know true deliverance when you can come in contact with that which you would have easily succumbed to before and emerge from the test victorious. The problem that many people face is that they get upset when they come in contact with even a weak dose of their struggle and realize that they have not been delivered from that thing just yet. In essence, they begin to feel a sense of guilt as if they have somehow let God down when, in all actuality, they should be thankful that God did not allow the true test before they had developed the strength to say "NO." You see, we can easily discipline ourselves from that which we do not like and those things which do not appeal to us; it is the things that attract us that make it hard to remain disciplined. This is why we must respect the process and be honest with ourselves about where we are in relation to our deliverance.

I am convinced that part of the reason why we struggle so much with the process is because of the expectations that we allow people to place upon us. We find ourselves looked down upon, shunned, even ridiculed, if we do not fit the image others have in their heads of who we should be. When we do not measure up to those standards, we so often feel like the process is tedious, painful, and filled with more disappointments and setbacks than results. It is important to remember that your process is just that, *your* process. Do not allow anyone to hold you to standards which they are likely not to even meet themselves. You know where you are, but more importantly, God knows where you are as it pertains to your deliverance. Unlike people, he will not give up on you. He is taking you through whatever you are experiencing for a reason. You were not meant to be an overnight sensation or a one hit wonder, and this struggle will ensure that you are built to last. Discipline plays a vital role in teaching you how to act, but it is the level of deliverance that is gained from going through and surviving the process that helps reveal to you who you are. You learn things about yourself during the process that you otherwise may have never known had you not gone through it. Allow it to teach you. Let it make, mold and shape you into everything that God intends for you to be. It will be so worth it when you come out of it on the other side in victory.

The process of refining gold that is impure involves putting it through the fire to get rid of everything that hinders it from reaching its greatest beauty. The process gets rid of things like copper, silver, iron, all of which serve a great purpose in their own right but ultimately prevents it from being gold in its most valuable state. What is keeping you from reaching your highest worth? The fire that you may be in right now is not to kill you; it is to burn the things off of your life that are stopping you from shining. It is to refine you through a process that shows just how valuable you are to God. He is not allowing you to go through the fire because he does not love you. He has not abandoned you, but just like the three Hebrew boys, he is walking with you, even in the midst of the fire. You shall not be consumed, but instead you will come out of your furnace of affliction better than when you first went in. Job says in 23:10 (KJV): "But he knows the way that I take:

When he has tried me, I shall come forth as gold." Be encouraged on today. God knows where you are going. Not only that, he knows where you have already been. Not even your process, no matter how long it has been, is enough to make him ashamed of you. He is leading you, guiding you, and sometimes even trying you, but you shall come forth as gold. Your story is not over. In fact, it has only just begun. Embrace the process. Real gold stands out from the fake stuff, but it would look just like all the rest if it had not gone through the fire. What you are facing right now are not simply "growing pains" but they are "glowing pains." After the fire, get ready to shine. Prepare to stand out in ways where you will not even look remotely close to anything like what you have been through. Embrace your process. Your deliverance is drawing nigh.

"If you quit on the process, you are quitting on the result." — Idowu Koyenikan

"For his anger endureth but a moment; in his favour is life: weeping may endure for a night, but joy cometh in the morning." Psalms 30:5 KJV

Chapter Eight:
Favor After Failure

～

Have you ever felt like you failed God? Like what you have done has been so bad that it is beyond the point of forgiveness? Have you ever slipped up to the point where you felt you had fallen so far that you were even out of the reach of an all knowing, loving Savior? Well, I have news for you: You are not alone. Many people today, good people, leave church because of a slip up — all because they feel like their failure is too costly for them to ever be fully restored. I cannot tell you the countless people that I have counseled and ministered to who have come to me expressing how they have felt too ashamed to even talk to God in prayer, all because they have done something that makes them feel as though they are not even worthy to come before his presence. But what if I told you this: That even before the mistake, long before the setback ever occurred, God *knew* that you were going to fail? Jeremiah 1:5 (KJV) says: "Before I formed thee in the belly, I knew thee; and before thou camest forth out of the womb I sanctified thee, and I ordained thee a prophet unto the nations." *Knew* in this context means two things: One, it means that he chose you. Before he even created you, God says that he already established intimacy with you by sanctifying you, setting you apart, and by ordaining you — meaning to consecrate, or anoint you. How mind blowing is that when you think about it in its full context? Before you were even a fetus in your mother's womb, God's perfect will had already chosen you. Then once you were created and placed in your mother's womb, he set you apart and then anointed you. So what then happened along the way to separate you from that intimacy, from that feeling of being called and chosen by God?

Adam and Eve, because of their disobedience to the voice of God, led us all to be sentenced to be born in sin. So the intimacy that was established in the womb with God became interrupted, and we were conceived with a "birth defect" in the form of sin brought into the world through our original mother and father. Just like a child today, we were born with certain qualities already embedded in us from the choices and decisions made by our parents. While we knew intimacy with God on the inside of the womb, once we were exposed to the world on the outside of that safe habitat of our mother's womb, we were then introduced to a sin nature that, through no fault of our own, we were simply made to inherit. So, as crazy as it may sound, God set you up to fail. He carefully and strategically orchestrated the fall so that unlike Adam and Eve, you would be able to see that you were not God, but that you needed someone to lead and to guide you, to catch you when you fell. Long before you were ever conceived he arranged a failure for you to experience that would teach you to rely on him, a loving and perfect God who cannot fail. The problem that I am convinced many of us face, however, is dealing with the failure after we have been born again. To be born again simply means to be born from above. This is of course a spiritual transformation whereby the believer receives eternal life. Being born of the water and of the spirit, we become the children of God by trusting in the name of Jesus, so what our previous Father Adam and Mother Eve did no longer holds us in bondage. Romans 8:15 (KJV) says: "For ye have not received the spirit of bondage again to fear; but ye have received the Spirit of adoption, whereby we cry, Abba, Father." It is under this adoption by Jesus Christ that we begin to celebrate the favor of God on our lives, and, alas, everything is seemingly OK. We are walking on the path of righteousness, running into love, joy, peace, and blessings and then one day it happens. Temptation arises and meets us head on and just like that, we have failed again — only this time it is far worse. We immediately begin to say to ourselves: "If I can't hold on after all these years of being saved, with this entire Bible that I know, all these thousands of prayers that I have prayed, then I may as well give up." We condemn ourselves, and we reach the conclusion that the favor that we once rejoiced in having over our lives now must surely be gone for good. "It is one thing to mess up and to sin while we are in the world," we say. But to fail after we have been walking under the umbrella of the goodness and mercies of God becomes unacceptable in our eyes, and we feel as though it is surely impossible to find favor once again in his sight.

Have you ever known anybody who holds a grudge? Someone who, even after years have passed since the wrong was done to them, no matter how many times the offender has apologized, they just cannot let it go? If that person is you reading this right now, then just say "Ouch." You can try and try to make it right, but they are just content and sold on the fact that no matter what, they are going to be angry about it, even if it is just the smallest thing. Can I share some refreshing news with you as you read this chapter right now? God is not like that, not in the least bit. In fact, Psalms 30:5 (KJV) says: "For his anger endureth but for a moment; in his favor is life: weeping may endure for a night, but joy cometh in the morning." Read the second part of that first clause again: "In his *favor* is *life*." Did it say in your *failure* is *death*? No, it does not. While The Bible does say in Romans 6:23 (KJV): "The wages of *sin* is death," by no means does it say that the wages of *failure* is death. His favor remains even after your greatest failure. God does not hold grudges. He does not stay angry. The Psalmist says "his anger endures but for a moment." He cannot stay angry with you because he loves you too much. Now, please allow me to interject something right here. While

God is a forgiving, loving God, until we stop alluding to how wonderful sin is we will never stop sinning. Like most people, I will admit that my sin was not miserable in the least bit, and I enjoyed what I was doing while I was doing it. But you will never be able to detach yourself from failure until you stop celebrating the pleasure that the sin brought you, and instead focus on the misery of the regrets. We oftentimes wait for something terrible to happen to us in order to scare us out of sin. But the worst consequence that you can have, one that probably seventy five percent of people deal with and do not even realize it, is the consequence of wanting something that you've already experienced, but are no longer permitted to have. It may be something you once enjoyed and still have access to, but you now know it is not good for you. It is not permissible.

The good news is that there is hope. I don't care how much of a failure you feel like. It doesn't matter even if you are in a backslidden condition. Remember the parable Jesus told about the prodigal son who enjoyed all of the favor that came with being in his father's house, only to mess up and to fail badly. But in spite of everything that he forgot when pride filled his heart, once he came to himself, he remembered how to get back home. You can never appreciate direction until you know what it means to have been lost. Regardless of what he had done, once he made it back home, without hesitation his father received him back and favored him by giving him a ring and a robe. In Luke 22:32 (KJV), Jesus tells Peter: "But I have prayed for thee, that thy faith fail not: and when thou art converted, or restored, strengthen thy brethren." Jesus foresaw Peter's failure before it had even taken place, but it did not matter because he had already forgiven him before he committed the sin. Yes, Peter, the foundation, the rock of the church, he too experienced failure, even denying The Lord three times. He got weak and he failed, but the love and the prayers of The Master Jesus Christ assured him that he would receive the favor that he would need to later become the mouthpiece of the Apostolic voice. You, who are reading this book right now, may feel like a failure and have tears running down your face as you turn the pages. You have stopped struggling, but that is only because you are no longer even putting up a fight. You are ready to retreat and run because of the war you have encountered for so long. But God wanted me to let you know that you do not truly know what warring is until you are dealing with the flesh and the spirit at the same time. If every time you fail you give in and you stop trying to embrace the spirit man, how will you ever recover and be restored? Give God a fighting chance today by praying even when you don't feel worthy of praying. Stir up the gift of God on the inside of you knowing that he will never abandon you, and that the very moment in which you fail, he is right there, imploring you to get back up and keep fighting. You learned your lesson, now move forward. There IS favor after your failure.

"Success is not final, failure is not fatal: it is the courage to continue that counts." — Winston S. Churchill

"When I discover who I am, I'll be free." —Ralph Ellison

Chapter Nine:
Identity Crisis

I recently received a text message from a close friend. It included an image which, initially, I found great humor in. But upon further examination of the picture, I noticed a sobering reality. The picture showed Batman standing all alone with what appeared to be a can of spray paint, and, with no witnesses to be found, he was writing on a brick wall these words: "Superman is Clark Kent." Although both are fictional characters of course, one hero was, for reasons unbeknownst to anyone besides himself, exposing the identity of another for the world to see. After getting a good laugh at this for a few seconds, suddenly the significance of this image dawned on me in a way that made me sit up in my chair and begin to take note. We are all aware of the major issues that confront us as believers today — things such as pride, lust, greed, just to name a few. But we are told in Song of Solomon 2:15 (KJV) that it is "the little foxes that spoil the vines." In other words, it is those issues that we so often are quick to just brush off and end up leaving unresolved, which so often lead to our downfall. Those "silent killers" as I like to call them, have a way of causing us to do things which threaten to sabotage not only our own identity, but to make us feel as though we have enemies that do not exist in the form of people who ultimately mean us no harm at all. One of the greatest of these issues that many of us deal with each and every day, battling it on the inside while smiling on the outside, is *insecurity*. One definition of insecurity is: the state of being open to danger or threat; lack of protection. It has a way of making you feel like so many people around you are a threat. More importantly, you become a threat to yourself, and a lack of confidence makes you go to extreme, often unreasonable, lengths to protect yourself. It is as old as Cain and Abel, Moses, Gideon, Peter, and so many more who all dealt with an insecurity that threatened to stop them from ever discovering their own true identity in Christ.

Hurt has a way of causing you to forget who you are. In a football game, when a player has suffered a head injury they are typically put through a series of tests to evaluate their recognition and their memory before they are permitted to return to the field. This "concussion protocol" can determine just how hurt they are. For instance, if they cannot recognize the coaches or teammates surrounding them, or how many fingers an individual may be holding up, then they may not be able to play again for weeks, even months. They cannot play until they are cleared by a neurologist and it has been determined that they no longer have any lasting effects from the injury. Have you ever been hurt so badly by life that it shook you to the core, up to the point where you lost your ability to think, even to see straight? If you live long enough, you will experience a pain that has a way of paralyzing you to the point of affecting not only how you see things around you, but how you view yourself. Some blows are bad enough and hit so hard that many people spend the rest of their lives trying to recover and in doing so, continue to sink further and further into a crisis brought about by losing touch with their identity.

The Bible says that Satan comes to do three primary things: "To steal, to kill, and to destroy." The first thing that he is intent on doing is "stealing" your identity, simply because he knows that if he can keep you from knowing who you truly are, then it becomes easy to kill, and ultimately, to destroy your position in God. When you are not aware of your identity, you develop a defeated mindset which makes it impossible to get but so close to your deliverance. Every time you feel like you have overcome something, you are confronted by and reminded of that which happened to you that made you unsure of yourself. It is that thing which keeps you up at night telling you that you are not good enough, that you will never be able to rise from the ashes under which you were buried and left for dead, and discover that you are more than a conqueror through Jesus Christ. But it is time to let today be the day that you do just that. Through the power vested in you by the Holy Spirit, you have the ability to reclaim your identity and to declare that you are the head and not the tail, above and not beneath, the lender and not the borrower. It is time to not only tell the devil who you are but to put him in his place, and tell him who he is as well and that he will no longer have dominion over any area of your life. The only reason your identity is under such heavy attack is because the enemy knows that once you discover who you are, you will recognize who he is — a liar who has tried to keep you bound by thoughts of insecurity. He knows that the confidence gained from knowing not only your place in God, but recognizing the power that you have, will render him and all of Hell helpless and powerless against you.

Now I find myself sitting here once again looking at the picture sent to me by my friend, and, once again, I catch myself laughing. Only this time it is for a different reason. I laugh now because I realize that even heroes like Batman are not immune to going through an identity crisis. Superman was not a threat to him, but the insecurity caused by somewhere along the way forgetting his own power, perhaps even becoming envious of the attention that his counterpart was receiving, caused one hero to forget who he was. It caused him to lose sight of the fact that he was equally as important and regarded just as highly as Superman. Something caused him to lose sight of his own identity. It can happen to anyone. Even as a pastor and preacher, having ministered to thousands of people, there have been times where I have found myself having to avoid becoming focused on what someone else is doing, not getting distracted by whose ministry is bigger or what the next man or woman may have. I have had to learn how to stay in my own lane and to be the best that I can be at that which God has called me to do. In doing so, I have come to realize that you learn how to truly value yourself because you realize, when you look back over all that God has brought you through, that your greatest strength, much like Superman, was not found in a cape, or by being "faster than a speeding bullet" or "able to leap tall buildings in a single bound," but it was revealed in the "phone booth." It was revealed in those quiet places where you were all by yourself, where you saw the battle ahead but you prepared for the battle long before it started, paying a price that only you could pay. So whether you are the target of someone else's struggle with their identity or you find yourself dealing with your own, know this: True greatness cannot be exposed, but in due time, it has a way of revealing itself. Thank God your identity crisis has been averted.

"Sometimes we fight who we are, struggling against ourselves and our natures. But we must learn to accept who we are and appreciate who we become. We must love ourselves for what and who we are, and believe in our talents." — Harley King

"You may encounter many defeats, but you must not be defeated. In fact, it may be necessary to encounter the defeats, so you can know who you are, what you can rise from, how you can still come out of it."—Maya Angelou

Chapter Ten:
When the Thorn Remains

As you may have gathered from reading the first nine chapters of this book, I have experienced quite a few highs and have trudged through the valley of the lows even as I have walked with God for all of these years. The one constant that remains, however, is something that I am sure you can be a witness to even as you process these words right now: There is power in prayer. In fact, I am going to take it one step further and say that there is power not only in prayer itself, but there is nothing that can quite compare to the joy and relief that comes to the soul than that of *answered* prayer. Particularly after you have gone through some of your toughest tests and withstood some of the hardest battles of your life, to talk to God and to know that he hears your cry by bringing you out and delivering you from the hand of the enemy has a way of increasing your faith and causing you to trust in him in an even greater way than you did before. But what happens when the exact opposite seems to occur? What happens when you have prayed over and over again about the same issue, only to find yourself still at war with the very thing that you thought surely by now God would have delivered you from? It can not only be demoralizing, but it can cause you to take a step back and to question whether or not your requests are being heard, or if deliverance will ever come your way. To know that God loves you is one thing, but it becomes increasingly difficult to understand how, with all of his might and strength, he can continually allow you to experience such moments of weakness and shame from dealing with the same painful cycle for what seems like an eternity. The thing that I have come to realize is that weakness is standard equipment on every human model.

We live in a culture and society today which demands that you hide your weakness. In this era where getting the most likes on Facebook leads to social media superstardom, you are looked down on and frowned upon for even the slightest hint of weakness. This, in turn, leads to people trying to hide, dismiss, and minimize those weaknesses with the hopes that they will eventually just fade into oblivion and go away. The truth of the matter, however, is that none of us, from the preacher in the pulpit, to the sinner in the back of the church, is exempt from having flaws and weaknesses. In fact, it is often those who are expected to be strong who are actually at times the weakest due to the demands and the expectations that are placed upon them. You would be surprised at the number of leaders who are responsible for helping people be strong but who are also dealing with their own spiritual kryptonite — things that leave them feeling weak. They are charged with the unenviable task of lifting up others who are hurting even while they themselves are in pain. Many times I tell young ministers who are wide eyed and ambitious about becoming pastors, not to discourage them, but to prepare them, that this is not a glorified or glamorous job. It is going to *cost* you something. There is a price to be paid to carry a mantle that requires you to be strong, but it also is not without its moments of great weakness as well.

There have been times when I have rejoiced with someone because I had helped them regain their strength when they were right on the verge of giving up. There have also been instances where I have shed tears because that same person turned their back on me and left me in a place of vulnerability and weakness from the heartache and sting of betrayal that cut so deep. No matter your stage in life, I am certain that you can share countless stories of finding yourself in a weak place where seeking The Lord diligently was the only option that made sense.

"When I am weak, then I am strong." It is these eight words from Paul recorded in 2 Corinthians 12:10 that, at first, jump out as a bit of a paradox. How is it possible for one to be both simultaneously weak *and* strong? The truth is, most of us are at that place in our lives right now. Indeed, it is not something for you to be ashamed of, but rather to discover God's purpose for your life, even in the midst of the weakness that you may be experiencing. Paul, a man of great strength and courage who endured more than most of us will go through in a lifetime, talks in great detail about his sufferings in 2 Corinthians 12:7 (KJV): "And lest I should be exalted above measure through the abundance of the revelations, there was given to me a thorn in the flesh, the messenger of Satan to buffet me, lest I should be exalted above measure." Paul was dealing with a dilemma that is all too common in the lives of you and me as believers today. He was trying to understand both the "why me?" and how God and Satan could be at work in his life at the same time. On one hand, he knew that the thorn was given to him by God for a sanctifying effect so that he would not become proud and that he might be able to move forward. Then on the other hand, there was "a messenger of Satan" which made things a bit confusing. When we know something is God's doing, then we can simply ask him to get the glory of out of it, and when we know Satan is at work, we can put on the whole armor of God and resist him. But the complexity of it being both at the same time requires strength as we continually learn that the flesh and the spirit are always at war.

It is the weakness of continuing pain that usually bothers us the most — especially after we have made our petition known to God over and over and the hurt still manages to linger. The words spoken by an alcoholic parent in our adolescent years that still weigh heavy on us and sting well into our adult years, affecting the psychology of who we are today; the reminders of trying to be a good husband or wife yet constantly being made to feel like our best was never good enough — some pain sticks around. Try as we may, we cannot understand why, but even the most fervent of prayers do not allow some things to just go away. It is these "thorns" which remain, after the tears, after all of the prayers, that leave us hurting and in need of answers. Paul, concerning his own thorn, said in 2 Corinthians 12:8 (KJV): "For this thing I besought the Lord thrice, that it might depart from me." While I don't know what Paul's particular thorn was, I know that it was extremely aggravating, especially if, having endured everything else this was the only thing that he asked to be relieved of. According to 2 Corinthians 12:2 (KJV), he said that this revelation was given to him fourteen years ago; this pain had continued up until this point of his life for at least fourteen years. Continual pain has a way of taking its toll on us and leaving us weak. We can be delivered from a number of different things, all of which we give God thanks and praise for, but it is often that one thorn that remains. It's that thing which hurts the most and strikes right at the heart of our deepest fears and insecurities that still cripples us and leaves us wondering why God, who is rich in mercy and grace, will not simply take away the very thing that brings so much pain into our lives.

Paul asked God to take away his thorn three times in what was not just a random prayer, but he pleaded with God and he still did not remove it. Throughout different seasons of his life, he still had to carry this thorn with him. As great of a preacher as he was, as strong as his relationship was with The Lord, he still had a thorn that he was not delivered from — a weakness that, in spite of his prayers, still remained. What do you do when the thorn remains in your life? Do you give up and feel as though you are a failure who cannot be used by God because of your reoccurring moment of weakness? Do you allow the pain of your thorn to cause you to retreat from your destiny? Do not allow your experience of weakness to make you believe that you are out of the will of God. The thorn remains in your life for a purpose far greater than what you are able to see right now. It is there to teach you to rely on God. "When I am weak, then I am strong." The Bible says that even Jesus was made perfect through his sufferings. He prayed for his thorn to be removed by asking that the cup be passed in the Garden of

Gethsemane, but God did not do it because his purpose for Jesus had to be fulfilled. The same goes for you. God hasn't removed the thorn from your life because it is a part of your purpose. In fact, dare I say that it is the greatest part to your story. That through your weaknesses, your flaws, faults and your shortcomings, God still looks at you every day — broken, hurting with tears streaming down your face. He looks at you and says give them to me just the way that they are, with the thorn included, yet to be fully delivered, and still, watch the glory that I get out of their lives.

> *"It isn't as bad as you sometimes think it is. It all works out. Don't worry. I say that to myself every morning. It all works out in the end. Put your trust in God, and move forward with faith and confidence in the future. The Lord will not forsake us. He will not forsake us. If we will put our trust in Him, if we will pray to Him, if we will live worthy of His blessings, He will hear our prayers." —Gordon B. Hinckley*

> "The struggle of life is one of our greatest blessings. It makes us patient, sensitive, and Godlike. It teaches us that although the world is full of suffering, it is also full of the overcoming of it." — Helen Keller

Chapter Eleven:
A Struggle Worth Celebrating

Many of you may be adjusting your eyes right now to try to determine if you read the title of this chapter correctly. Struggle? Celebrating? I know those two words certainly do not seem to go together. But before you say to yourself, "Dr. Walker must be exhausted from trying to meet his deadline for finishing this book," let me assure you that your eyes are not playing tricks on you and that this is not a misprint or a typo. For far too long, I feel as though we have incorrectly defined what deliverance truly means. Not just people, but *good people*, are leaving our churches at an alarming rate because they have been made to feel as though deliverance means that any semblance of struggles that they had before coming to Christ should completely cease to exist. Therefore, they often fall short of the expectations of those who have a "religious" mindset and, as a result, before they can even birth their destiny they suffer a "spiritual miscarriage" that negatively affects their relationship with God. But whether you were just delivered from a life of sin five minutes ago, or fifty years ago, allow me to redefine what that truly means. Deliverance does not mean that you do not have a struggle. It simply means that you have your struggle under control. Paul put it like this when he wrote these words: "Brethren, I count not myself to have apprehended: but this one thing I do, forgetting those things which are behind, and reaching forth unto those things which are before" (Philippians 3:13, KJV). Deliverance is acknowledging that you may not quite be where your purpose is leading you to, but that, even in the midst of struggle, you can celebrate the level of victory that you have already achieved, while continually striving for more.

I do wish to make it clear that I am by no means downplaying the significance of holiness. I am completely aware that The Bible

A Struggle Worth Celebrating

says in Hebrews 12:14 (KJV): "Without holiness no man shall see The Lord." I am simply stating that, the pursuit of holiness requires us to sometimes maneuver through the pathway of struggles. There are strongholds in our lives that we deal with for years which have taken root in our minds, and they do not suddenly go away the very moment that we come to Christ. No one becomes a finished product overnight. In fact, a *rushed* product is often a *ruined* product. Discipline takes *time,* and getting to a place where you can say that you are fully delivered can take a *lifetime.* I dare even take it a step further and say that it is possible that you can die with certain struggles that go with you, even unto the grave. Sure, it is customary for the preacher to stand before your family and friends and to give an eloquent eulogy about how wonderful a person you were as they all gather together to celebrate your life at a funeral. Most of the people in attendance, however, would cringe and squirm in their seats if they only knew your struggles, and the innermost secrets that you never told anyone about. Those things, to them, certainly would not warrant celebrating. No one throws confetti for a struggle. The cake and the punch are typically reserved for those who have arrived, not those who are still navigating their way around obstacles, scratching, clawing, and fighting to make it, sometimes even looking hopeless and in despair. But thank God for a Savior who sees things differently — one who is still ready to celebrate us, sometimes even in the midst of our greatest struggles.

"And not only so, but we glory in tribulations also." These words from Paul in the opening half of Romans 5:3 seemingly go against the grain of conventional wisdom and would certainly appear to, at first glance, throw any semblance of logic out the window. By definition of the word, to *glory* in something means "to take great pride or pleasure in." So what Paul is essentially saying is that we are to be proud of what we are going through. Not only that, but he phrases it in such a way that lets us know that the celebration is not to be reserved for *after* we have endured the struggle and come out victorious. By saying "we glory *in* tribulations also" he is suggesting that even during our greatest tests, right in the midst of them, we should rejoice. For good measure, he even includes the word "also" to serve as an admonition to us that just as we find joy in our triumphs, likewise we should do the same in our tribulations, "knowing that tribulation worketh patience (James 1:3, KJV); and patience, experience; and experience, hope." So as difficult as it is to see during the moment when we are faced with our greatest struggles, the things that they teach us and equip us with mean that ultimately, they are working for our good.

Picture if you will, a prize fighter. Here he is, in the fight of his life. He looks battered, bruised, one eye swollen shut, blood trickling down his cheek, struggling just to stay on his feet with every blow to the body and the face that he absorbs. He is tired, swinging almost blindly, unsure if he is still even connecting with his opponent. Yet through the exhaustion, he manages to glance at the clock, and he sees that he is in the last seconds of the final round. He doesn't know it, but he is winning on the scorecard. All he has to do is endure and stay on his feet and the result, in a matter of moments, will be that he is crowned champion. Yes, the struggle has been real. You can be sure that the knockdown in the previous round, the pain that he felt made him contemplate staying down the last time, but he remembers something. He remembers that this was what he spent hours in the gym preparing for; this is what he dreamed of his whole life, up until the time when he was an amateur boxer just getting his feet wet. And though it may be a struggle, even to make it through fifteen more seconds which feel like an eternity, he is not about to allow any degree of pain, any amount of struggle, to keep him from capturing the ultimate prize. Again, he looks up at the clock as the crowd stands to their feet cheering him on... Five, four, three, two... He raises his hand as he walks back to his corner being greeted with sheer exuberance and enthusiasm by his trainer and all those on his team who know the work, the blood, sweat, tears, but most of all, the *struggle* that it took to get to this moment where inevitably, he will be announced as the winner, and the celebration will ensue.

Allow me this opportunity to present you with some great news. You are not defined by your struggle. Instead, when you come through all of the trials that you have had to go through, you will be celebrated because of your struggle. You have gone blow for blow, toe to toe, with some of the most difficult challenges of your life, yet you have survived. The average person would have lost their mind with the struggles you have had to face, but God has equipped you with purpose. 2 Timothy 3:5 (KJV) says:

"Thou therefore endure hardness, as a good soldier of Jesus Christ." Disciplined, but not delivered, you keep enduring. You are an unfinished product in the eyes of God, but he still sees you as His Masterpiece, struggles and all. That sounds like a great reason for celebration to me.

> *Challenge is the pathway to engagement and progress in our lives. But not all challenges are created equal. Some challenges make us feel alive, engaged, connected, and fulfilled. Others simply overwhelm us. Knowing the difference as you set bigger and bolder challenges for yourself is critical to your sanity, success, and satisfaction.* — Brendon Burchard

"Where you start is not nearly as important as where you finish."
— *Zig Ziglar*

Chapter Twelve:
Finishing the Course

As I sit down to write this final chapter, I also realize that I have actually come to a conclusion in a chapter of my very own life. I have been blessed to experience fifty years here on this earth, but as strange as it may sound, it was only recently that I actually became an adult. Having just completed eighteen years in ministry, the process of discipline has in all actuality, led me to experience a level of discipline that I did not know I had reached. If you will, recall in the previous chapter that I said: Deliverance does not mean that you do not have a struggle. It simply means that you have your struggle under control. It may take time, and it may seem at first to be an act done out of religious obligation, but one thing is for certain: Discipline will eventually create an invisible boundary, one which only the heart is able to see. Whether discipline or deliverance, you can only claim either based off of that to which you have been exposed. It has often been said that there is no teacher quite like experience, and while this does indeed hold such great truth, there are valuable lessons to be learned from inexperience as well. Without the experiences you do not know your limitations, and with inexperience comes not knowing your full ability and what you are able to accomplish. The key is found in learning this valuable lesson from both the experiences and the inexperience: You do not begin to truly live until you free yourself from trying to do that which is impossible — living up to the expectations of other people.

Take Joshua for example. He did not enter into the promise land when he first went there to spy out the land because the people, due to their inexperience, did not believe that they could win the battle against the giants. Therefore, Joshua had to rely on his own experiences and reflect on the battles that had already been won by God in his life. Those experiences gave him confidence and the knowledge that, regardless of how big the giants were in Canaan, nothing was going to stop him from entering into the land that was flowing with milk and honey, even if it meant that he and Caleb would have to go alone. It is crucial along your journey, as you navigate through the course of life somewhere between discipline and your deliverance, that you do not allow other people's perceptions to become your reality. Regardless of what they have seen and the lens of fear that has caused them to want to retreat from the giants in front of them, you have to know, based on your faith experiences, that you can defeat your giants and not allow anyone or anything to throw you off course and cause you to wander back into the wilderness from whence you came.

Indeed, this course that you are on is a personal one. When Paul made his announcement of departure, he spoke these words which epitomized the near conclusion of a journey for a man who had been beaten, stoned, ostracized and criticized and left for dead, all in the name of Jesus Christ: "I have fought a good fight, I have finished my course; I have kept the faith" (2 Timothy 4:7, KJV). I imagine him fighting back tears, reflecting on his life ever since his encounter with Jesus on Damascus Road, realizing that by no means had it been easy, but at the same time being unwilling to trade anything for his journey with Christ along the way. "I have finished my course"... Again I say, it's personal. On his journey to Rome, he told the passengers with him on board the ship that God had promised them that they would reach their destination. But shortly after speaking these words of assurance, a storm came, and they found themselves shipwrecked. What do you do when you have been told that you would make it to the end of your course safe and sound and life throws you a shipwreck? What do you do when God promised you would make it out of your storm and you find the "pieces" of your deliverance broken and scattered all around you? You do exactly what these prisoners did when their ship wrecked. The Word of God declares in the book of Acts 27:44 (KJV): "And some swam, some on boards, and some on broken pieces of the ship. And so it came to pass, that they escaped all safe to land."

The point that I am trying to make is this: We are all aiming for the same final destination — eternal life with Jesus Christ. We will not all get there the same way, but what matters is not how you get there, but simply that you get there. You may be broken, in need of deliverance like never before, but use those broken pieces. Use those broken pieces not to hold on simply to stay above water until you inevitably sink and drown in despair, but use what you have to help you reach your destination. It may not seem like much at first glance, but strengthen that which remains. Once you have been to the extremes of both good and evil, you learn to find the balance that God originally intended for you before you decided to lend a hand to his handiwork. Somewhere along the way, we all hopped off of the potter's wheel and decided to attempt to reshape ourselves into what we wanted to be, leading to our need for deliverance. Much like in chapter one when Adam and Eve heard God's voice walking in the garden and hid, you and I have tried to hide too long from the shame of being disciplined, but not delivered. Today, it is time to make up in your mind, once and for all, that you are no longer going to hide. God is saying: "Come out, come out, wherever you are." He wants to restore you back to the original glory that He intended for you in Eden. It is time for you to say: "God, here I am, flaws and mistakes, brokenness, and all. I'm exposing *myself* so that you can reveal *yourself* in my life in a way that you never have before." Final course, final chapter: Revelations. May the grace of God be with us all.

"God would not bring you through a Red Sea and turn around and allow you to perish in a fish pond." —Johnnie Dent Jr.

CPSIA information can be obtained
at www.ICGtesting.com
Printed in the USA
FFOW05n1028110216